Bedtime Prayers & Lullabies

TWILA ✿ PARIS

Paintings by
Kathryn Andrews Fincher

HARVEST HOUSE PUBLISHERS
EUGENE, OREGON

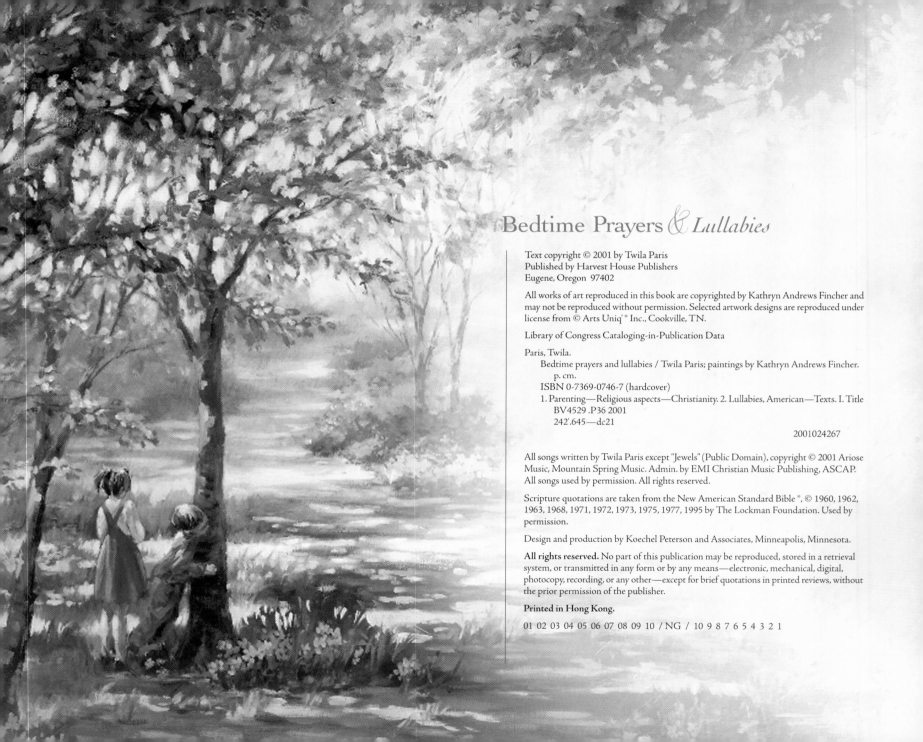

Bedtime Prayers & *Lullabies*

Text copyright © 2001 by Twila Paris
Published by Harvest House Publishers
Eugene, Oregon 97402

All works of art reproduced in this book are copyrighted by Kathryn Andrews Fincher and may not be reproduced without permission. Selected artwork designs are reproduced under license from © Arts Uniq'® Inc., Cookville, TN.

Library of Congress Cataloging-in-Publication Data

Paris, Twila.
    Bedtime prayers and lullabies / Twila Paris; paintings by Kathryn Andrews Fincher.
        p. cm.
    ISBN 0-7369-0746-7 (hardcover)
    1. Parenting—Religious aspects—Christianity. 2. Lullabies, American—Texts. I. Title
    BV4529 .P36 2001
    242'.645—dc21

                                                                    2001024267

All songs written by Twila Paris except "Jewels" (Public Domain), copyright © 2001 Ariose Music, Mountain Spring Music. Admin. by EMI Christian Music Publishing, ASCAP. All songs used by permission. All rights reserved.

Scripture quotations are taken from the New American Standard Bible ®, © 1960, 1962, 1963, 1968, 1971, 1972, 1973, 1975, 1977, 1995 by The Lockman Foundation. Used by permission.

Design and production by Koechel Peterson and Associates, Minneapolis, Minnesota.

Printed in Hong Kong.

01 02 03 04 05 06 07 08 09 10 / NG / 10 9 8 7 6 5 4 3 2 1

Lullabies *from* My Heart

When I wrote these lullabies, the dream of having children was something I had released into the Lord's hands several years earlier. I had come to the point of realizing that I needed to make peace with whatever God's will was for my life—even if that meant never having a child of my own. The prayer that my husband, Jack, and I prayed was not "God, give us a baby," but "God, may Your will be done in our lives."

Even though I had no children of my own, the dream of writing an album of songs for children had been with me for some time. In the past year I determined it was finally time to do just that. So over a period of several months, I sat down and wrote these songs for other people's children. As I wrote, I felt that the Lord was giving me a special heart for children and an anointing to share some important truths

through a collection of lullabies. Sometimes tears would well up in my eyes as I penned the words and imagined the little ones with whom I could share these precious truths.

Just weeks after I finished writing these songs, I received some very exciting news: Jack and I would soon have a baby of our own. It has been a long wait and we are very grateful to God—as well as very excited! We are expecting our new baby shortly after this book is released. The book, the album, and the baby will all be arriving at about the same time! Little did I know when I first began this project that I would be singing these special songs to my own child.

My goal in writing these words and lyrics is not simply to offer songs that will aid children in falling into a peaceful sleep or help them find moments of restful peace during the midst of their day. My larger purpose is to gently instill foundational truths in young, vulnerable minds, to help children understand how God feels about them. It is my way of drawing them close to my heart and whispering, "Here is what I want you to know: God made you very special. He loves you and will always take care of you. He has a very special destiny in mind for you if you will follow Him." I want children to understand the great privilege of knowing Him, of walking with Him, and of telling others about Him.

In the simplest sense, these songs represent the things I want my own child to know about God and about His love and care for him. I believe they are the things you'll want your child to know as well. I decided that in the pages of this book I'd take the opportunity to speak to the children (and the child in all of us) through the simple text that accompanies the illustrations, and also to address parents with some thoughts about how we can help our children to make these truths real in their own lives. I believe the basic principles

here are just as relevant for adults as for children. These foundational truths are the heritage we have to share with our children and pass down through the generations. David wrote, "The lines have fallen to me in pleasant places; indeed, my heritage is beautiful to me" (Psalm 16:6). As parents we have a beautiful heritage of faith to pass down to our children. I want to cement these truths solidly into the heart of my child while he (or she!) is still very young, because these are the truths that stay with us. They are truths that we can know at the deepest level of our heart, not just as an idea in our head. They will be a guide and companion to us all through our lives.

We all need someone to share the excitement and sanctuary of faith with us. I am the product of a family consisting of a long heritage of preachers and Bible teachers. From my earliest days, my dad and mom taught me about God and His love for me. They sang lots of lullabies, and every night at bedtime one of them would read from *Hurlbut's Story of the Bible*. And with their own lives they modeled what love looked like. But they were not the only ones. My grandmother, who lived next door, sometimes gathered up the children of the neighborhood and told us Bible stories, often even acting them out with the cardboard cutouts on her flannel graph. She was not only a student of the Word, but a fabulous storyteller as well. She'd raise her voice and, in her native Arkansas accent, she'd launch into a dramatic retelling of one of the Bible stories. The truths I learned sitting on the floor in her front room are truths that have stuck with me. I hope that in the pages of this book I can do for your child a little of what that wonderful lady did for me.

What a privilege it is to be able to share with you the simple truths these songs teach. I hope they prove a blessing to your family and provide some wonderful moments together for you and your child.

Twila

Good night, little one.

As you close your eyes to rest awhile,

I want to remind you how much I love you,

And how very much God loves you, too.

There Is Only One

For You formed my inward parts;

You wove me in my mother's womb.

I will give thanks to You, for I am fearfully

and wonderfully made;

Wonderful are Your works,

And my soul knows it very well.

My frame was not hidden from You,

When I was made in secret,

And skillfully wrought in the depths of the earth;

Your eyes have seen my unformed substance;

And in Your book were all written

The days that were ordained for me,

When as yet there was not one of them.

PSALM 139:13-16

There is only one person like you

In all of this great big world

And you are just who God

made you to be

Whether a boy or a girl

Whether you are black or white

Or some beautiful color in between

No matter your shape or size

You're as perfect as anything

I've ever seen

Your mom and your dad

They are so glad

You are part of their family

There is only one

Who loves you more

He is Your Father in heaven

He is the Lord

Sometimes our children struggle with the way they look or their family background or something else that makes them different from other kids. When you are young, it is hard to feel different from everybody else. And let's be honest, sometimes as adults we still struggle with such feelings. We want so badly to fit in at work, at church, or with the expectations of those around us. But we need to remember, and we need to teach our children, that it is okay to be different.

Our uniqueness is part of God's plan. The things that make us different from others are not a mistake or oversight on God's part. Your child is just who God intended him to be. He made your little one to be uniquely who he is, with his own part to play in God's eternal design. God made him different from everyone else because He has plans and dreams for your child that no one else can fulfill. As parents, we should help our children to respond to God's unique call on their life. As my dad always taught me, "If God puts a dream in your heart, He'll give you the ability to follow it."

One way to encourage our children to be who they are is to help them remember that ultimately it is only God's opinion that really matters. My dad always used to say that true success comes from combining my faithfulness with God's faithfulness. We are each given the gifts and talents we need to accomplish what He has in mind for us. And He does have something special for each one. ✤

*You are so very **special, Little One**, there's no one else like you.*

Curly hair or straight, eyes blue, brown, or green,

***God made you** just the way He wanted you to be.*

*So as you fall asleep, remember that **God thinks***

***you are "just right"** (and so do I!).*

Your Whole Life Long

For this boy I prayed, and
the LORD has given me my
petition which I asked of
Him. So I have also
dedicated him to the LORD;
as long as he lives he is
dedicated to the LORD.

I SAMUEL 1:27,28

*I pray the Lord will hold you close
And keep you through the night
That you will wake up smiling
In the early morning light
That He will always comfort you
And make you brave and strong
I pray that you will follow Him
Your whole life long*

*I pray that you will grow up
To be wise and good and true
I pray that you will please the Lord
In everything you do
I pray that you will hear His voice
And learn to sing His song
I pray that you will follow Him
Your whole life long*

*I pray the Lord will bless you
With His presence every day
And I pray He will protect you
Every step along the way
Help you love what's right
And lead you far away from wrong
I pray that you will follow Him
Your whole life long*

As I am writing this book, Jack and I are awaiting the birth of our first child. We feel like the biblical character Hannah did when she heard she would bear a son: God has done a great miracle for us. Jack has been reminding me lately that we can't think of this as *our* child. This little one is the Lord's, and He has a very special plan and purpose for this child. He has entrusted us with helping our child come to a living relationship with Jesus and grow strong in his faith. Our job is to receive this gift with open hands and to be good stewards of the awesome responsibility we have been given.

The words of this song represent my heartfelt prayer for my baby. I want him to discover God's love and to walk in that love his whole life long. Sometimes, as parents, we can feel kind of powerless, unable to steer our child into God's path even by our best efforts and our most passionate and encouraging words. But the one thing we can always do for our children is to pray for them. We can entrust them to the only one who loves them even more than we do. For they truly do belong to Him. ✾

Little One, you're so *small* that I can hold you in my arms, But *someday* you'll be *as big* as me. Then you'll *follow Jesus* and walk with Him *all your days*. So as you fall asleep, remember *how proud I am of you*.

More Than I Can Say

The One who makes the children
Is watching from above
He placed you in a family
So that you could know His love
A mother and a father
To hold you here on earth
But He was with you long before
The moment of your birth

And if you don't have a mother
He will sing you lullabies
And He'll be right beside you every day
When you're all alone at night in bed
If you feel like crying, it's okay
He will wipe your tears away

The One who hears the children
Has known you from the start
He placed you in a family
So that you could feel His heart
A mother and a father
To keep you safe and warm
But He was with you long before
The day that you were born

And if you don't have a daddy
He will be your father, too
And He will always keep you in His sight
When it gets too dark to see ahead
And you can't find your way
It's still all right
He will be your guiding light

He loves you
More than I can say
And He is always taking care of you
He loves you
More than I can say
And more than I can say
He hopes that you will love Him, too

God gave us families as one of His ways of showing us how much He loves us. They are a concrete demonstration of His caring. Through his parents, a child first learns what it feels like to be loved.

One of our major tasks as parents is to teach our children, through our words and actions, how very much they are loved by God. The part we play in their lives is so important. We offer them security and guidance, in a certain sense representing Him with what we say and how we live. We are models and examples, teachers and instructors. Of course, we will never do a perfect job of showing the fullness of love that our children need. Sometimes we'll be impatient and angry. Other times we'll be inattentive and selfish, caught up in our own set of needs and priorities.

But although we are not perfect, and never will be, we should remember that we have an awesome responsibility to be a living example of God's love. This should not be something that stresses us out and makes us feel overwhelmed. Instead, we do our best, trying to follow God's leading and trusting His strength. God will fill in the gaps. We can rest easy in the Lord, because we know that He makes up for what we lack in parental skills. Or, if you are a single parent, worried that you can't do the job alone, you can rest in the assurance that God has promised to be a Father to the fatherless. He never fails. For He is the perfect Father, the One who knows how to love us—and our children—just as we need to be loved. ❧

My sweet one, I love you more than you can know.

Every time I think of you *I smile*.

But Jesus loves you even more.

So as you fall asleep, feel *His love.*

My Delight

Delight yourself

in the Lord; And

He will give you

the desires of

your heart.

PSALM 37:4

When I learn to listen
Follow where You lead
You will keep me satisfied
Give me what I need

When I learn to love You
Keep my heart on fire
You will be my everything
All that I desire

I will wait to hear Your voice
I will look into Your eyes
I could search around the world
And never find a greater prize

My delight
You are my delight
I think about You
Day and night
You are my delight

One of my favorite movies is *The Sound of Music*, and one of my favorite scenes is when the children are all huddled together in Maria's bed during a thunderstorm and she gently sings to them the song "My Favorite Things." You remember her list? It included things like raindrops on roses, whiskers on kittens, bright copper kettles, warm woolen mittens, and brown paper packages tied up with string. These are the things that Maria took delight in. They made her smile all over.

But as wonderful as things like these are, nothing brings such lasting joy into our lives as our relationship with God. David knew that, and he wrote about it in Psalm 37. He had discovered that there is no delight like spending time with God. And the wonderful reality is that God loves to spend time with us!

Spending time with God is a little bit like spending time with our friends. If we don't see them very often, then our times together can feel a little awkward and uncomfortable. But when we are together often, the relationship deepens and grows. We get past the small talk and into the deepest kind of sharing. It is like that with God. If we make the time for Him in our lives and teach our children to do the same, we will learn that the moments we spend with Him can be our favorite moments of our whole day, our deepest delight. ✤

The world is full of wondrous things,

Things that make you laugh and make your heart sing.

But nothing is as wonderful as knowing Jesus.

So as you fall asleep, delight in Him.

My Best Friend

A man of too many
friends comes to ruin,
But there is a friend
who sticks closer
than a brother.

PROVERBS 18:24

Jesus is my best friend
I can always go to Him
Tell Him everything
I'm dreaming of
My friend Jesus
Whom I love

Jesus is my best friend
He'll go with me 'til the end
Watching over me
From up above
My friend Jesus
Whom I love
My friend Jesus
Whom I love

What would life be like without friends? Wouldn't we be much poorer if we did not have people in our lives about whom we care deeply and who care deeply about us? What is there that can compare with spending time with a dear friend? Our human relationships mean so much to us, adding joy and meaning to our days. But even our best and most trusted friends cannot always be counted on. Sometimes they will let us down or disappoint us. Maybe they just can't be there for us when we need them most.

But there is One who is always there, who always loves and cares for us, who always wants the best for us, and will always lend a listening ear. We must keep our eyes on Jesus, the One who is our very best friend. He delights in spending time with us because we are created for fellowship with Him. He is with us when we are awake and when we are asleep. Even when it seems that no one understands, He knows our hearts and sees our deepest potential. He is a friend like no other.

When we introduce our children to Jesus, we are introducing them to a friend who will be with them for life; someone who can be with them even when we can't. He is the one true companion who will never let them down. From our children's earliest days, we should teach and model the importance of spending time with Him. That is probably the single greatest key to helping them grow in their relationship with the Lord. Friendship takes time to develop and mature. As we guide them in special times with Jesus, they will find the joy of having a friend who sticks closer than a brother. ❧

As you grow, many people will love you,

Friends who are kind and true.

But even when no one else is there, Jesus will be with you.

So as you fall asleep, you can talk to Him.

God Is All Around Us

The heavens are telling

of the glory of God;

And their expanse is

declaring the work of

His hands. Day to day

pours forth speech,

And night to night

reveals knowledge.

PSALM 19:1, 2

The sun behind the mountain
Is setting in the west
The bluebird and her little ones
Are gathered in their nest
And I am on my pillow
Because I need my rest
God is all around us
And He knows best

He's higher than the treetops
In the tallest wood
Why He would come and speak to me
I'd tell you if I could
It makes me want to please Him
In all the ways I should
God is all around us
And He is good

God is all around us
Everywhere we go
Caring for His children
That's all I need to know

He's stronger than the eagle
Circling above
He's wiser than the oldest owl
More gentle than a dove
He's closer than pajamas
That fit me like a glove
God is all around us
And He is love

I remember once, while visiting near El Paso, Texas, being absolutely blown away by the beauty of a desert sunset. There were no trees in the way of the horizon and the sky was immense, streaked with fiery orange, yellow, and bloodred clouds as the sun sank behind the mountains. It was an awesome moment.

I've traveled a lot and seen many sunsets, but nothing compares with watching the sun go down in Arkansas, where I live. Arkansas sunsets are a little less dramatic, a little cozier, but still gorgeous. I often find myself standing in awe as the evening sun slants through the trees in my own backyard and am filled with wonder at the overwhelming splendor, yet truly at home.

Whenever I experience this kind of beauty, my heart naturally responds in praise. For God created everything, absolutely everything. And though beauty wasn't necessary—you cannot point to any practical reason why God made this world so breathtakingly beautiful, so full of glorious colors and stunning vistas—God's artistry is in evidence everywhere we look.

Wherever our eyes may settle, we see the work of God's hand, the signs of His love all around us. Nature is filled with principles and parables that reflect His goodness. If we are attentive to its "voice," it reminds us how great God is and how small we are. It tends to put everything in perspective.

We would do well to introduce our children to the glory of the outdoors, the wisdom hidden in the wildness. We can teach them to be more attentive, to slow down and notice the little things around them, like the flight of a butterfly or the leaves changing color in the trees. If they spend most of their days in the rush and bustle of city life, it would be good for them to get an occasional lungful of fresh forest air or a drink of cool water from a mountain stream. And to be reminded that the God who created *everything* stoops down low enough to embrace us in His love. ✤

Little One, you're such a **small person**
in such a great **big world**,
But **God** shows His **power** in all that He has made
And His **love in caring** for every little thing.
So as you fall asleep, **be thankful** to Him.

Jewels

Jesus…said to them, "Permit the children to come to Me; do not hinder them; for the kingdom of God belongs to such as these. Truly I say to you, whoever does not receive the kingdom of God like a child will not enter it at all." And He took them in His arms and began blessing them, laying His hands upon them.

MARK 10:14-16

When He cometh
When He cometh
To make up His jewels
All His jewels, precious jewels
His loved and His own
Like the stars of the morning
His bright crown adorning
They will shine in their beauty
Bright gems for His crown

Little children
Little children
Who love their Redeemer
Are the pure ones
Are the bright ones
His loved and His own
Like the stars of the morning
His bright crown adorning
They will shine in their beauty
Bright gems for His crown

Jesus adored children. I can imagine Him having a twinkle in His eye whenever they were around. He'd laugh with them and let them climb up on His lap. He loved having them around as a reminder of the nature of God's Kingdom.

"Jewels" is the only song I recorded for my lullaby album that I didn't write myself. But it is a song with a special place in my heart. I loved to sing it when I was little. In fact, when I was four years old, I recorded a special custom album and included this song on it. Although I don't think I was old enough to fully understand everything the song said, I knew it was about children and how much Jesus loved them, how proud He was of them. I understood that by pleasing Him with godly actions, I could add to His glory, becoming a gem for His crown. I loved the imagery of His bright crown and wanted to be one of the pure ones, one of the bright ones who reflected His light. I wanted to make Him happy by the way I chose to live my life.

We can't do anything to make Jesus love us any more or any less, but we sure can make Him happier by the choices we make in our lives. It is important that we help our children learn to recognize the voice of their conscience from an early age. To learn to listen to that inner voice and be obedient to what God has spoken in His Word. For our obedience and purity bring glory to Him. They make us shine like jewels!

Jesus loves all the little children, just as He loves you.

He wants to show them how to be happy,

By living their life the way He wants them to.

So as you fall asleep, know that He cares for you.

Bedtime Prayer

Now I lay me down to sleep
I pray, dear Lord, that You will keep
Your eyes upon this sleeping world
Every little boy and girl
Bless the children far away
The ones who don't know how to pray
Those who are not feeling well
The little one who slipped and fell
Bless the puppy down the street
The neighbors I have yet to meet
Bless my mom and dad especially

Just one more thing I'd like to say
Before I close another day
I'd like to thank You, Lord
For all the ways You bless me

Bless the child whose home is torn
The babies who are not yet born
Bless the ones who take Your Word
To all the hearts that have not heard
Bless all Your children everywhere
I hope they know how much You care
Maybe someday I can go and tell them
That You love them so
Bless Grandma and my grandpa too
And all my friends and all they do
Bless every twig upon my family tree

Just one more thing I'll say to You
I'm so amazed by all You do
I thank You once again
Because it's true
That You bless me

I wrote "Bedtime Prayer" to teach little ones about thoughtfulness and selflessness and gratitude; to help young hearts recall the many ways God has blessed them and to remind them to pray for the needs of others. Don't we all want our children to develop the virtues of thankfulness and a compassionate heart? To do this, we need to teach them to look outward, beyond their own needs and into the needs of others. Our task begins with finding creative ways to help our children connect at a heart level with the hardships of others. We can point out items in the news, talk with them about the struggles of friends and neighbors, and show them God's heart for the suffering. Our goal should be to increase their awareness.

One way to do this is to get them involved in actually doing something to help others. For example, last Christmas I took some little friends of mine to a temporary children's shelter, a place for abused children with no place to go, who would have to spend the holidays in the shelter. We called ahead and found out the ages of some of the most needy kids and then went shopping to buy them special presents. The kids had so much fun picking out just the right gifts! Then, on Christmas Eve, we delivered all the presents. What a joy it was for the kids to have the opportunity to make an impact on other young people's lives in this way.

Or consider sponsoring a child through an organization like Compassion or World Vision, letting your children help you pick out a child to support. On my last tour, a large family came to sign up after the concert. Because money was pretty tight for them, they decided that they'd have to give something up so that there would be enough money for the sponsorship. The kids huddled together for a moment and decided that once a month they would forgo their tradition of having lunch out after church so they could afford to sponsor a child. They have learned by experience how their actions and prayers can work together to bring hope and help to others. ❧

There are children tonight who are sad and crying.
They don't have all the good things you've been given.
Some of them don't know how much God loves them.
So as you fall asleep, dear child, pray for them.

Perfect Peace

The steadfast of mind You will

keep in perfect peace,

Because he trusts in You.

Trust in the LORD forever,

For in God the LORD, we have

an everlasting Rock.

ISAIAH 26:3,4

Do not be afraid, little lamb
Trust Him while you are sleeping
Angels over your cradle will stand
Silent watch they are keeping
Think about these things
And love will guide your dreams

You are never alone, little lamb
For the Father is near you
You are tenderly held in His hand
Whisper and He will hear you
Think about these things
And love will guide your dreams

And He will keep you in perfect peace
Perfect peace
Perfect peace
He will keep you in perfect peace
If you keep your mind on Him
If you keep your mind on Him
So keep your mind on Him, little lamb

There is no more helpless feeling than watching a child you love go through pain that you can do little or nothing to alleviate. We want to be able to "kiss it and make it better." But sometimes we realize there is little we can do. Except pray.

My nephew, Mikey, was born last April with a genetic condition requiring intensive surgery when he was only two days old. He came into the world missing the connection between his esophagus and his stomach. Rushed into the operating room, he underwent the necessary repairs, then had to spend a month in intensive care. For a whole month the complications of the surgery left him unable to cry, unable to eat, and with great difficulty in breathing. It was obvious that he was in pain. But he had no way to express it. He couldn't make a sound. So we, and many friends all over the world, began praying for him.

We knew he was hurting, but there was no way to explain it to him. And because he was hooked up to so many tubes and monitors, we couldn't hold and comfort him the way we wanted to. But what we could do was pray that God would give him peace.

I wrote these lines in the song especially for Mikey: "You are never alone, little lamb / For the Father is near you / You are tenderly held in His hand / Whisper and He will hear you." When I first played this song for my sister and her husband, I could hardly get the words out as my eyes filled with tears. Over the course of that month I watched and prayed and witnessed what it means to have peace that passes all understanding. God moved in a special way for that family.

And by six months old, Mikey was a fat and happy baby boy. There was no question about the quality of his vocal cords! And here is what I learned: If we focus on our problems, we will be anxious. If we focus on Him, we will find His peace. ❧

Remember, little lamb,

That God is always watching out for you,

Even when you hurt inside, He is with you.

So as you fall asleep, be at peace.

See You Tomorrow

Early in the morning
I open up my eyes
Before I even touch the floor
I look up to the sky
And I say thank You for this day
I want to make You happy
All day long

You are my Father
And I love You
I'm glad You made the sky so blue
You are my God and I will praise You
You made the sunrise
I'm glad You made me, too

Last thing in the evening
When I am all tucked in
And I am thinking peaceful thoughts
Because of You, my friend
And I say thank You for this day
Please forgive the things that I did wrong
I'm glad when I am weak
That You're so strong

You are my Father
And I love You
I'm glad You made the stars so bright
You are my God and I will praise You
Before I fall asleep
I'd like to say good-night
See You tomorrow

Some of the lullabies in this book are addressed to a child. Others, like this one, are written as though from the mouth of a child. As the psalmist reminds us, even the very young can offer up praise and worship to God. Sometimes, during a church service, I'll notice little kids, maybe only four or five years old, standing on a chair or pew during worship and lifting their hands with their eyes closed, just worshiping God. This always touches me so deeply. Even if they don't fully understand everything that's going on, they are learning the importance of praise. Children have the capacity to express openly their love and adoration in such a wonderful way. I think God loves the vulnerability of their little hearts.

As parents, let's try to encourage our children to put into words their love for God and their appreciation for all He has done for them. Children can learn to worship at a very early age. As they grow, give them opportunities in your time together as a family to pray and share their heart. I've seen God use even the very young in ministry, especially in the ministry of intercessory prayer. And let's never forget that God wants us all to come to Him with a childlike heart. ❧

When you wake up in the morning,

It'll be a brand new day to jump and play and dance and smile.

The God who keeps you tonight will walk with you tomorrow.

So as you fall asleep, know that you are held in His arms.

His
Beloved

I will bless the LORD who has
counseled me; Indeed, my mind
instructs me in the night. I have
set the LORD continually before
me; Because He is at my right
hand, I will not be shaken.

PSALM 16:7, 8

He gives to His beloved
Even in their sleep
He pours His hope and wisdom
From streams that run so deep
He promises to help them
His promise He will keep
He gives to His beloved
Even in their sleep

He sings to His beloved
Songs of peace and rest
He loves His little children
And gives them all the best
And those who learn to trust Him
Forever will be blessed
He sings to His beloved
Songs of peace and rest
He sings to His beloved
Songs of peace and rest

When I was writing songs for my last album. I found myself emotionally and creatively drained but under the pressure of a looming deadline. I still needed a couple more songs to complete the project. I was feeling very anxious and worried, so Jack gently prayed for me just before I fell asleep one night, asking that God would give me peace and creativity. The next morning I woke up very early with a song rattling around in my head. I went to the piano, sat down, and was amazed as the words to a powerful song just seemed to come tumbling out. Though it came to me so quickly, that song has been one that many people have said touched them deeply.

I shouldn't have been surprised by this experience. My dad often told me that when he had a problem or was deeply worried about something, he would pray about it at night just before he went to sleep and that very often he would wake up with the answer. The Lord would minister to him while he slept.

This is such a powerful reminder that God is always with us. Even as we sleep, God speaks to our hearts. He gives us counsel and guidance, helps us sort out what really matters in our lives, touches us with His peace and comfort, or gives us strength. That's why it is so important to remember to pray before we go to sleep and to teach our children to do likewise. Taking the time to pray with your children every evening, asking them about anything that might be bothering them, is a way to help them feel more at peace. Praying just before we go to sleep sets us off in the right direction on our journey of slumber. And the God who loves us never slumbers, never sleeps (Psalm 121:4). ✿

As you sleep, my little child,
Remember God stays awake to care for you.
I pray He will give you rest.
So as you fall asleep, have the sweetest dreams.

Blessing

The LORD bless you, and
keep you; The LORD make
His face shine on you,
And be gracious to you;
The LORD lift up His
countenance on you,
And give you peace.

NUMBERS 6:24-26

May the Lord bless you and keep you

And may His face shine upon you

May the Lord bless you and keep you

And give you peace

May the Lord bless you and keep you

May He be gracious unto you

May the Lord bless you and keep you

And give you peace

Grace and peace

Grace and peace

May the Lord give you peace

Grace and peace

Grace and peace

Always

Always

Recently I spoke with a woman who told me that her dad prayed this blessing from the book of Numbers over her and her brothers and sisters every morning before they climbed aboard the school bus. I thought it was a wonderful idea to send them off into each new day with a blessing.

I actually wrote this song, based on Numbers 6, for my little brother's wedding. During communion I joined my sisters in singing it as a blessing over the couple's new life together. Then later, when my nephew was struggling for life in the neonatal intensive care unit (where he spent the first month of his life), my sister and her husband sang it quietly to him every evening. And God did shine His blessing into this painful situation, bringing hope and healing to this young family.

These words from Scripture capture what every parent hopes for their child, no matter how young or how old. God's blessing. God's favor. God's grace. God's peace. And it is so important that our children hear words of blessing come from our mouths and that we be the channels through which this blessing is given, a sign of our love for them and trust in God.

I pray that the Lord will always bless you,

That He will look on you with a smile,

That you'll always know His grace and peace.

So as you fall asleep, precious gift,

be blessed.